WHISPER OF SPLENDOR

Poems by Chong Hyon-Jong

Modern Poetry from Korea Series
Published by Homa & Sekey Books

Flowers in the Toilet Bowl: Selected Poems of Choi Seungho

Drawing Lines: Selected Poems of Moon Dok-su

I Want to Hijack an Airplane: Selected Poems of Kim Seung-hee

What the Spider Said: Poems of Chang Soo Ko

A Love Song for the Earnest: Selected Poems of Shin Kyungrim

Sunrise over the East Sea: Selected Poems of Park Hi-jin

Cracking the Shell: Three Korean Ecopoets: Poems of Seungho Choi, Chiha Kim, and Hyonjong Chong

The Dream of Things: Selected Poems of Hyonjong Chong

Translucency: Selected Poems of Chankyung Sung

Our Encounter: Selected Poems of Kyu-Hwa Kim

Blue Stallion: Poems of Yu Chi-whan

Belly Button Disc: Selected Poems of Dongho Kim

A Lion at Three in the Morning: Poems of Nam Jin-Woo

SF-Consensus: Poems of Park Je-chun

Whisper of Splendor: Poems by Chong Hyon-Jong

Whisper of Splendor

Poems by Chong Hyon-Jong

Translated by Cho Young-Shil

Homa & Sekey Books
Paramus, New Jersey

FIRST EDITION

Published by arrangement with Moonji Publishing Co.

This publication was supported by a grant from the Literature Translation Institute of Korea (LTI Korea).

Library of Congress Cataloging-in-Publication Data

Names: Chong, Hyon-jong, author. | Cho, Yong-sil, translator.
Title: Whisper of splendor : poems / by Chong Hyon-Jong ; translated by Cho Young-Shil.
Description: First Edition. | Paramus, New Jersey : Homa & Sekey Books, [2018]
Identifiers: LCCN 2017052198 | ISBN 9781622460458 (pbk.)
Subjects: LCSH: Chfong, Hyfon-jong--Translations into English.
Classification: LCC PL992.2.H6 A2 2018 | DDC 895.71/4--dc23
LC record available at https://lccn.loc.gov/2017052198

Published by Homa & Sekey Books
3rd Floor, North Tower
Mack-Cali Center III
140 E. Ridgewood Ave.
Paramus, NJ 07652

Tel: 201-261-8810, 800-870-HOMA
Fax: 201-261-8890
Email: info@homabooks.com
Website: www.homabooks.com

Printed in U.S.A.
1 3 5 7 9 10 8 6 4 2

The Poet's Note

In the splendor of loneliness and tears
Splendor of shadows and breast
Splendor of breaths and winds

Table of Contents

Time Blossoming 1

Behold the waves of Time
It's morning
Already tomorrow morning
Sailing on this very night
to meet another day
my waves
are blue, oh so blue
their undulation
tinges the light of every day;
oh the heart,
where dawn rises

Poetry Came Surging and Surging

Poetry came surging and surging
while I slept;
the world is but a window
or the egg called the earth
whose beak is now cracking it open
or time is a perpetual
pulse of ethereal daylight,
poetry as such surging over anyhow
the universe with some blue ether
the light for which nothing is impervious,
infinity smiling, formed by that light—
the infinity right in my eyes
the infinity suffusing my whole body
poetry as such still surging over anyhow
yet I chose to sleep on
instead of arising to set it down...
(it may well be that I no longer think
it'll be lost unless put down,
that the egg will hatch just the same
in the bosom of slumber)

Time Blossoming 2

All of us in this age,
I'd say, we've lost Time long ago
Let us consider: truth is,
we bustle around
in thrall to money and machinery
spending Time like cash, like stuff,
apparently never feeling Time itself!
so one wonders what's become
of Time itself, the very flower of it
The posy blows only when we ponder on it—
without its fragrance, or the nostrils
inhaling the fragrance,
then our life and this world are mere oddments;
none but a poetic mind will see this rare flower and
its hour blossoming
hence we must be total wrecks
living without knowing of our own wreckage
in this world already wrecked

O My Hearts

This day is so fair
dusk is in its own color
sky in its own color
clouds in their own color
and these are the cumulus clouds
that I used to see as a child
O my hearts—
twilight-heart
sky-heart
cloud-heart
O heart of its own color

Scarlet Ivy Runners

The ivy runners have so soon turned red!
Isn't life worth living, my heart
throbs along with these scarlet runners!
The scarlet spirits of pomegranate and apple
and of all flames flock over
to paint them so;
all spirits of the world's heart
at once invade
and together with the spirit of time, the spirit of
change,
the spirit of wind, ruffle the leaves
to color them so;
isn't life worth living, scarlet ivy runners,
the world's heart,
O my heart

Each to Each

To be fuel, each to each,
that's the supreme way!
(Kindle a fire in me,
and I will in you)
All things
through fire undergo flux.
(Heraclitus, for certain,
seized on fire.*
If you will seize on something, let
it be no less great than this at least)

* Heraclitus, a Greek philosopher born in 535 BC, propounded that all things constantly change, and that fire is an element of the world.

An Ailing Friend's Earth

When my friend had a surgery to remove stomach
    cancer
I threw a brake on the earth's velocity.
Then I
ceased to go out larking,
and could tell the earth was now spinning slower.

Some Solitude

Suffering a brief lonely spell
wild flowers you gathered
and twined into a bracelet.
Boundless was the time spent in silence
the round thing, inside and out, full of solitude.

You wore it on your wrist
or left it on the table
and I, in your absence,
look upon the floral bracelet lying there.

Upon it converges the universe
and loneliness pervades without end.
In that air I too at once
am kindred with the solitude—
together with the hand that brought it.

A Day

A day is ten thousand years
a moment veritably an aeon.
Where does the day end?
It never ends.
Somewhere the sun rises
somewhere it sinks.
(Just as love rises then sinks)
Heat knows no end.
Nor do ashes.
The wind's chest is limitless
and so are the river's sighs.
The sky with all its folds
the heart with all its chambers
so goes laughter endless
as do tears.
No way to contain the body heat of the whole of crea-
tion
infinity unfolds, channels its course full to the brim.
The sky with all its folds
the heart with all its chambers,
a day never ends.

A House Built of Air

In a valley in Yangpyung, I was told,
Kim Wha-Young had built himself a house
so I pay a visit;
but no house here,
only so much clear air
Maybe his building material was air
Whether sitting or lying down,
coming in or going out,
one perceives air for floors, air for doors,
and air for walls
The more hardships
and conflicts in the construction,
all the more air
for the abode
Sprawling on the ground is a sylvan god
breathing through the lungs of the valleys

Ode to a Cricket

It is all very well Autumn came but
O cricket you're making a sound
underneath my desk,
though not quite like a stone step,
so intent
on and on without a break
pouring into my ear
your clear music
your pure sound
O cricket
you're letting flow
from my ears
a spring that never dries out
and the clearest in the world,
your sound
vibrating from the wings
on a tiny, 17-millimeter body
arousing me from my summer-long sloth
and the mind prone to be slothful
is a Word which, let us say,
the sacred texts of all those so-called religions
put together
could never be anywhere near; O better singer
intent, purposefully intent,

pouring your word into my ear
until I grasp
(in truth, I did upon hearing)
and turning my heart
into a wellspring
of the world's clearest spring-water
O you a better singer

O Art!
—Venetian Poems 1

I lodged at a monastery
in the isle of San Georgio, Venetia.
Arose in the morning, stepped out
and gazed up at the holy edifice: there,
the leafage carved in relief
each blossom tossing aloft.
Those leaves for hundreds of years
have shored up this ponderous edifice
and upon them I slumbered!
And upon those blossoms!

O aesthetic will just barely salvaging
this hefty history;
carved leaves and
flower relief,
upon these indeed I slumbered last night.
Just barely salvaging my dreams,
O art, O aesthetic will!

The Creation
—Venetian Poems 2

When God the Creator created everything
He did so by becoming the very thing.
He flew with the bird
when creating a bird,
ran with the dog
when making a dog,
swam with the fish
when creating a fish
as seen in The Creation of the Animals by Tintoretto.*

(The best way of all creations)

* Jacopo Robusti Tintoretto (1518-1594) was an Italian painter during the Renaissance period, who painted this masterpiece circa 1550, based on the Biblical account of the Creation.

Those Lucent Clouds

Nine in the evening.
Ate out supper
with a glass of wine,
on the way back home
happened to look up at the sky, and ah
clouds are great masses of light
and the sky cerulean on this evening.
Might even die
on account of white lucent clouds.
Again I head for the bar.

Taking shower at home now, ah
what should bathe me but those same clouds!

Blunders

I
perhaps reproach myself 'excessively'
when I've erred
so please don't scold me too hard

Besides, John of the Cross
called excess of self-reproach
yet another kind of imperfection
(clearly, I say, a barrage of blunders)

Where the Wind Rises

A day's come to nothing
because of a woman.

A day's come to nothing
because of liquor.

(oh heart, oh body, how dreadful to be heavy)

There's a fruit called the mind.
And a fruit called the body.
Surely the two are
compost and sunlight
and wind to each other

oh earth,
on a windless day
you can never shake off your own heaviness
Is woman a wind—
Is liquor sunlight—

But as ever
the heart remains the sky,
where the wind rises.

A Fine Day

This day's light so bright, so fine
my brow touches a cloud

Wind wafts
infinity all over me

Joy in the air
Hope in the day's light

Flower of the Sea

Flower of the sea,
the sea that is a flower
new-born camellias
cannot bear up.
Red, red
ever so red
but strangely powerless are they
before the flower of the sea.

Horizon

Lying on my side I see the horizon
through the window.
From head to toe
I too at once am a horizon.
Now two horizons
in parallel.

(A creature on earth,
the heart, always being a horizon,
ever moves along
with birds,
farther and farther along with birds,
so it's been infinitely forlorn)*

Lying on my side
by the sea
in parallel with the horizon,
by this serendipity
I am no mere giant
but a heavenly being.
Thus vanishing
into the universe.

*Refer to my previous work, “On the Wings of Horizon and Solitude”.

The Heart Where Dawn Rises

——Venetian Poems 3

February 3, 2005
I awake at daybreak
and Marco occupies my thoughts,
a student at La' Focari University of Venice.
(majoring in Chinese with a minor in Korean.)
In the first light
he guided me in a ship
from Piazza San March to the airport
and so sincere
was his attitude,
most probably
St. Marco himself incarnated.
The day is dismal
so, too, is desire
capital cruel
waves cold
yet beside me
is a warm spark burning up.
The epiphany
of St. Marco.

Poems I Write Hereafter

The poems I write hereafter
will not be in a poetry book,
all of them
I will fling to the wind
or somehow totally let go.
I sure will.
(Oh what a liberation.)

Fake Busy

1

Do not be actually busy
but fake busy.
That, to yourself only
fake busy.

2

Till your leisure
at last becomes windfall, take it easy,
take it easy to fake busy.

I Feel Sad

Supposing that by now
the one expected to come must've come
I feel sad.
Supposing that the one expected to leave must've left
I shall feel sad.
(Don't know why)
but over *all* those finales
I feel sad.

Enormous Unconsciousness

Life spells enormous unconsciousness.
And that is forever so.

A mom walks by, holding her little girl's hand.
Prattle-prattle, goes the little one
talk-talk, repeats the mom after her.
Who am I.
A thought flashes on me:
I am born of that little girl.
There's no beginning, no end, to it all.

Oh Stillness

Walking down
the path to the garden-slope,
behind a building
among trees I heard stillness
(maybe because this was a rare
moment when you don't hear cars, motorcycles, all
the noises from technological civilization,
or even people)
ah, it was stillness
that I suddenly heard!
Turning my head
continually in that direction to see
looking, and looking
all at once I am being restored!
Joy is brimming in me!
This modern world's best secret medicine,
Oh stillness.

Song for the Shoe Repair Shop

Those shoe repair shops
here and there in the streets,
people who come and sit there are always
peaceful.
The heart is overflowing—
Content to be watching
content to be sitting.
Maybe because it is small.
Maybe because it is lowly.
Maybe because there's no more sacred place than
those.
Maybe because at last we
are at our proper place.

Moving Packages

Moving packages,
all of the moving packages
are so utterly holy
I can't even cast a level glance at them.

Good Old Days

—The young Kim Seong-Yun's recollection

In my youth, I tell you,
I had nothing
no worry
no fear.
It was that way with friends
and with my teacher:
more than anything,
they all had the heart.
They bestowed their heart on me
told me to take it
to take it.
Those were really good old days.

Musicians

Bach

The seas overspreading the earth
The breakers
that are the breaths
of such thick substances
between heaven and earth,
their unceasing(!)
undulation bearing
divineness
peace and infinity
and
the dances
in motions
in faithful obedience

Beethoven

Thunder rolls
in the body
and the heart
sees tempests
Majestic,
august,

Titanic!
Now bursting
forth,
now towering
upright,
one colossus
and many more!

Mozart

All
the fountains
never going dry
on earth
(In truth)
diamonds
of sorrows
on earth
Many a voice in laughter
rising,
tears
gushing,
such
splendor
of cheerfulness!

Remaining Variation

Refreshing the heart
therefore

refreshing the body
so much as does Nature,
and besides
ever since the emergence of mankind
surpassingly
the greatest
of all blessings

Hell

This person
ever since his birth
turned his place into a hell.
And to lord over hell
he had to turn that place even more infernal,
for that is how to retain the hell
and what the power instinct does.

Who has no hell within him
but
if human in some measure
he will try not to spread his own hell
out into the world.
However, my topic here is not my own affair.

This person
shunned and hid from
the light of the day made by the sun, wind
and all hearts, and ah,
darkened the morning
and made heavy the evening.

The Hand Lifted in the Air

Solemnly moved
after reading Goethe's *Elective Affinities*
I
saw my hand
lifted in the air
before I knew it.
Already I
was staring at
that hand.

The heart's nature
(which is a serious play instinct)
glides past
the world's systems
and morals,
unfolds one by one
the hidden worlds,
and this relentless truthfulness
of one man
lets me be born again.

(That's the earth's rotation and revolution)

The hand
lifted in the air.

Oh Stillness 2

Scaling
a spring mountain
touching and touching
little buds
then sitting on the fallen leaves
and looking
upon the mountains
and valleys
yonder
all at once
the heart
grows still.
Still ever
so still.
(Be still, and
you shall live)

Oh endless
stillness.
Oh the heart's breathing flesh.

Scent of Soil

I took one sniff at the soil
then swallowed my saliva
and sweet
was the saliva!

The Mind Sprouts Everywhere

The mind sprouts everywhere.
Like a lightning it sprouts
from the rain-shiny leaves,
when the backdrop of a man passing outside the win-
dow
expands upon the seed of his own movements
it's ready to blossom,
and certainly from vibrant sorrow
and also heliotropic joy, the mind
sprouts.
No matter where, the mind sprouts.

Gait 9

There's someone walking, fearing the earth will give
under his feet.
A schoolbag in one hand
a shopping bag in the other—
This one anyhow seems so heavy-laden
O Ground, pray don't give way under his feet.

Infinite Exterior

When one walks out of his room
into the wood, how happy
to hear birds singing and wheeling on their wing!
Breathing the same air they breathe
you are thoroughly one with them,
sharing the same ground with them
your motion joins theirs,
all things in one flow
shaping an infinite exterior…

A Visitor

To have a visitor
is indeed a matter of gravity.
For he
brings with him his past
present
plus
his future.
Brings with him his whole life.
Brings with him his heart
vulnerable as can be
as may have been cut asunder — a heart
whose written account
a wind may be able to read;
should my heart imitate such wind
this visit after all will be a hearty welcome.

On Dignity

How hard to hold dignity
in this world.
Sometimes others mar it, but
sometimes we ourselves are the abdicators.
In talking about losing one's dignity
often we don't know
how much to blame ourselves
and how much others.
Ah still,
still!
Is it so hard
to think right!

Chimney

There's a chimney
stacked on my shoulders;
when I am heated
or when my chest fills with smoke
through this chimney I let it all out.
Sometimes my chimney puffs out thick smoke,
sometimes
just stays like an empty house.

(At all events I
recommend this chimney remedy.
And the chimney
will do better if pretty
say, like a quaint one at an ancient temple.)

Killing Poetry

One's ambition to write poetry
by itself
is enough to kill it,
says Henri Michaux!

Poetry,
you don't even starve to death.

Women

Well I know women.
That means I know what womanhood means.
Women are Nature.

We cannot but glory in
our Nature,
the paradise personified, said to be lost.
The matrix
which was
before history
before civilization
before me
before you,
or
as declared by André Breton:
"the corolla dripping with vowels."

It All Depends How You Make Up Your Mind

It all depends how you make up your mind.
Nothing will happen if you do not
but if you do
nothing will be impossible.

The mind's spontaneous imprinting
of those living things' shadows,
they too
are imprinted as they are
only after you make up your mind.

It is a fantastic thing to say
I make up my mind.
What do you say I do with my mind?
I say you make up your mind!
Then
nothing will be impossible, I repeat.

Once you make up your mind
then comes singing.
And dancing.
Once you make up your mind
you hear through the ear of all things
and see through the eye of all things.

Once you make up your mind
the pristine Mind
returns
and dawn comes on
in the dark.

A Note on Art

— Upon visiting the Orchid Pavilion in Shaoxing

I pay a visit to the Orchid Pavilion in Shaoxing,
where Wang Xizhi used to regale himself,
and watching gold fish swim in the pond
slap my lap, That's it!
What made him a master calligrapher
was these fish's motions
and
these tree-branches
crafting in the air their own calligraphic style
all they wish.

Morning

In the morning
there's no such thing as fate.
The only thing there is
is a newborn day
with fresh vigor!

Fate may
come near
lumbering
at nightfall or in the night,
but in the morning
there's no such thing as fate.

Wine Flavor

— Upon visiting the Orchid Pavilion in Shaoxing

Flavor in wine
is something determined by
your drinking pal
the time
the place
and the mood and atmosphere
all such things create.
The vital thing, however,
is artistic elegance.

The Orchid Pavilion
where Wang Xizhi regaled himself,
there in the waters
winding and flowing
they floated a glass filled with Shaoxing-wine
then with long-handled gauze scoop
ladled up that floating glass and offered;
so another glassful! I couldn't help myself.

Two Feiyans come alive*
graceful in their traditional costume
scooped the glass, as I asked,
offered it level to my breast

and I took upon my palms
these ladies too
and drank them up in one gulp.

Had they laid supine the letter 太(meaning great) superbly carved
on the stone monument erected beside
it would've been better.

*Zhao Feiyan became the royal wife of Emperor Cheng of the Han dynasty. She was so slight in build as to stand upon a man's palms.

What Vision!

Walking the slope of Mt. Cheonggye,
suddenly on a spot
I see a world awash in light!
Azaleas everywhere.
A world full of laughter,
what Nirvana alight is this!
What vision!
(All religions, ideas, philosophies,
what visions have they proffered…)
Were we to have this vision
we'll forever bloom;
with laughing air, laughing waters, laughing world
    over,
there'll bloom flower-light and light-flower.

A Contemplation

'Rice-cake dumpling' selected
as the subject.
Whether that person likes rice-cake dumpling or not…
We're to have lunch together…
Would he rather have fish…
I'd better ask.

A Constellation Walking About

— In praise of Park Na-Hee

Park Na-Hee, a student of astrophysics,
researcher of cosmic ray
of the energy coming from the universe into the earth.
(In a doctorate program, Astrophysics Dept., Eewha
    Women's Univ.)
Fascinated by constellations ever since childhood,
she has never lost a chance to sight a celestial body.
Loathing "the trend
that, if a sterling student, you're to go to a medical
    school,"
loathing therefore common notions and conventionali-
    ty
and social passivity!
she decided on 'real study.'
So from Vienna, Austria
she received the 'Young Scientist Award,'
perhaps an award from the stars
making my heart shine as well,
at any rate
to reject to be a stick in the mud
eager to unfold 'the mystery of universe,'
how splendid, how very splendid!
Shine; O star on this earth.

A heavenly constellation
walking about on the face of the earth,
isn't the earth the very heavens!

Wind Shadow

I look out the window.
There is a wind.

After some time, I look out again.
And still there is a wind.
It's been quite a while…
Swaying branches
swaying leaves.

The flicker on Time's face
deepens the wind's movements.
Shadows
flickering,
deep are the wind's movements.
For sorrow moves.

Sorrow moves.
The wind's shadow.

Oh the Warmth!

I bought a bag of roasted chestnuts, put it in my brief-
case,
got on the bus and laid it in my lap,
and now I have this warm feeling.

The warmth of chestnuts just roasted — instantly
I feel quite so happy.
The sun, home, fireside,
dearness, bosom, and then
this pilgrimage and...
Oh, all the warmth that there is,
the fountain of happiness.

Upon Visiting the West Lake (Xi Hu)
— Hangzhou poems

On the way back in a boat
after mirroring myself in Hoshindo,
the eyeball of the West Lake,
Sodongpa's landscape
with droves of tourists is nowhere to be seen
but I, one in that odious flood,
in the flurry of today's itinerary
improvised a poem, recited,
and the twenty four fellow travelers heard me.

Upon the body of Seo-shi*
have arisen twenty four moons,
(why the moon
always rises upon the lake)
at any rate
today the moons the color of white wine.

On this tour
(since I'm at it)
finally
the sphere, hard to attain as they say,
has descended to commonness,

so, well I may
stop here now.

* Sodongpa, in one of his poems, compared the West Lake to the beautiful Seo-shi.

Oh the Seeds

— On a high school anniversary

They carry their nickname 'Lively,'
these teen-age
boys and girls.
An infinity in motion
they are, so to speak.
An infinity of potentiality
an infinity of curiosity
an infinity of creativity
an infinity of concentration
an infinity of dreams....
A school plainly is a space
where you let all those infinite things
reach full flower
function well
ripen well;
where you inspire
and nurture
that their spontaneity
—the reserve unknown—
 should shine forth.
Anyway
the arms
that infinitely preciously

fold
the seeds
inside those children
(so translucent, so palpable).
You can hear
the seeds
breathing.

Tang of Energy

This morning
I'm having a green apple, an early crop,
and so rapt
over its green fresh flavor
my heart at once
dances.
Energy unbounded
in the freshness
the tongue savors.
The tang of
vitality
now in my mouth,
after all the flowing
and winding through
the labyrinth
of those dynamic resources
stored in Nature.
The heart dances
to the wavelength of light
O freshness.

O the Dazzle of Diamond

— Istanbul Poems

Topkapi Palace Museum's Treasury Section
The very moment you stand before
the 86-carat diamond,
a lightning of lights!
All gemstones are virtual suns
yet this enormous diamond is literally the sun itself!
To let your eyes fixate such luminescence
is dangerous, for you will be blind
or lose your mind.
O the stone so dazzling, you just gasp,
not a word, and certainly no creed
but a virtual light
O the dazzle of diamond.

Praise for a Mountain

Nostalgia
for a far mountain,
when faced closely
it is
armful
in my bosom!

When I scrape that mountain
rise up
higher and higher
along with the trees,
then air alone is my energy
and laughter my fuel!

Come down
and look upon it,
then I am already
a giant
incomparable to myself,
and a blue vault!

Light-Drops

— Music by Jin Eun-Sook

Dew of sound
drops of certain light
heaving
sparkling
rolling
bolt-striking
light-drops.
In the flesh
a reef of sounds — very likely
a gold mine of sounds,
the hand
that abstracts
and separates light
from all things anyhow
whether a wave
or a rock
or a bell ringing,
dewdrops of light
at the fingertips!

A Sacred Picture

Morning hours,
a café in the mountain,
all about the round table were seated Kim, Yee,
Oh, Cheong, Chae, Choi, Huh….and others;
through a large window the sunlight—pools of it
poured in illuminating
the round table; good heavens! a sacred picture it is,
as if Rembrandt, directed by Nature,
were working
the morning hours and
that bright clear light and
most of all, the round shape
(blessings on all round things!)
of the round table
were making that picture sacred.
That round table was a table
and a corona.
(Needless to say, sacred are
the laughter and tears
and anyway, lives of the figures in the picture)

Whisper of Splendor

The splendor
of the movement of Time
as the day draws to an end
in the gloaming
nothing wanting
so are solitude or seeds
one separate universe each
(which is splendor of all splendors)
could poetry, I wonder,
join in that movement.

Whatever sweeps over you when you secretly weep
for the loneliness of the ailing
could that be perhaps poetry.
(O splendor of loneliness and tears)

Underneath this ground still tracked
with all the past shadows of footprints
could poetry lay her breast somewhere there.
(Splendor of shadows and breast!)

The sky's windy edge still suffused
with all the past breaths

could poetry breathe somewhere there.
(O splendor of breaths and winds)

Shangri-La

In this I may be silly but
for me
every place I visit for the first time
is a Shangri-La.
Therefore
all along before I leave
my destination somehow feels dreamlike
and as departure day nears
I'm even slightly transported.
(Oh Time, oh seasons
who can live without transports)
Every place I visit for the first time somehow
is all Shangri-La—
My instinct for reverie.

Of Places

All places
must provide something vibrant.
Something vibrant provided, then
that's a place worth staying.
Be it a thing, a mind, or whatever
be it a sight, a demon, or whatever
if one doesn't encounter something vibrant there
that's no place.
(For instance, the heart in love vibrates with sudden
    live energy.
The sorrowing heart always lifts live energy.
An upright movement stirs in the heart a joyous fresh
    wind.)
If not vibrant enough for the mind to catch sudden
    fire,
vibrant enough to sprout the whole body,
vibrant enough to lift a cool breeze,
that's no place.
Oh the deadness of places.
Would we ever taste
a vibrancy in mankind's Time,
ever experience
such grace rare indeed….
Time's laughing, and sighing.

For, even so, poetry and other contiguous arts
MUST be the vibrancy of the place,
may our Time
and also our abiding places
be properly vibrant: this is the movement we make….

Commentary

The Poems That Dream of Infinite Light Waves

Park Hye-Kyung

1. Easy, light, and simple

Chong Hyon-Jong's poems in *Whisper of Splendor* (2008) are easy, light, and simple. No need to rack your brains out trying to grasp the poems' real meaning, you just feel them surge like waves or breaths and then sink smoothly into your mind. A feeling that the one you just read has gone right through you unseen and simply vanished, the poetic sweetness savored at the moment of reading still intact—just as soon as you take a full bite of cotton candy it dissolves formless, leaving the sweet taste in your mouth. This feeling is similar to the restfulness acquired after letting go of the mental attitude of clutching something. Further, it is a state ready to drop conscious effort to abandon this possessiveness. Chong's poems, with all the abandonment there is, surge on toward infinity beyond the consciousness still so possessive, toward that rhythmic, undulating 'nothingness.' This is why his poems are getting simpler.

What has sustained Chong's poems is his desire to empty out endless desires steadily loaded in the bundles of poetry and life. When he was fascinated by Nijinsky planting himself firm on his toes, or when he praised a springy ball, its taut air nearly bursting out of the leather, springing off the ground, he dreamed of the perfect lightness of the mind earth-bound but nonetheless unbounded by life on earth; also of the joy brought by the concentrated moment when the mind's centrifugal force, contracting then expanding by turns, tackles the earthly centripetal force. However, one can trace in his earlier poems a mental struggle for such state, or a strain caused by the struggle. One can thus perceive in those poems a decisive effort to draw things into tightly strained consciousness of the poet himself, who infuses full-blown poetic imagination into things, who oscillates between reality and dream, between pain and fascination. In short, his poems so far have focused not on things themselves but on rhythmic imagination they bred in his consciousness.

Since then, precisely since *There's Not Much Time to Love* (1989), however, his poems gradually tended to immerse in thingism, rather than in imagination's subjective rhythm for surroundings. Which means his attitude began to change from straining to draw things into the inner chamber of consciousness to committing self to the attraction of things. The poems in *Whisper of Splendor* also are an extension of such change. What stands out in this change is his eagerness to take out the tangled web of meanings that packs consciousness, so that he will take in things as they are, as they move. Now Chong chooses to empty out all his body and take in the hidden mystery of things whose waves or breaths are nonverbal messages to him. In other words, this was the inception of poetic rhythm that outreaches not to the ownership (*avoir*) of things but their state (*être*), not to the meaning of things but their being. In my previous critical essay on Chong Hyon-Jong's works, I portrayed this poetic rhythm as a state in which "consciousness reflects objects, objects functioning as the mirror of consciousness, so there's one whole movement with no inside or outside." It is a little child's innocence toward an object, delighting and marveling at its presence; or a world of lucid inclusiveness seeking the experience of initial encounter with the object, like a patient convalescing from a long illness and seeing the world with renewed wonder. Declining to translate things from outside and thereon construct their complicated meanings, Chong now wants a poetry in which he moves along with things. He renounces interpretive authority to impose meaning on things, and rather chooses to enter them as an innocent player. This is why his poems are getting easy, light, and simple. In this respect, my commentary here perhaps amounts to nothing but a pad that unnecessarily comes at the close of a poetry book. For it will be a futile attempt for me to wield structural meaning so as to constrain Chong's desire to flee from a meaning-driven, much-afflicted world. But then what? Imprisoned by words, we are but poor prisoners of words, and forever will be....

2. Daylight of the Infinite Exterior

The vocabulary words most often noted in *Whisper of Splendor* are 'undulation,' 'wave,' 'daylight,' 'infinity,' 'blue,' 'overflows,' 'winds,' 'rising,' 'gushing,' and so on. The following are good examples:

> Sailing on this very night
> to meet another day
> my waves
> are blue, oh so blue
> their undulation
> tinges the light of every day;
>
> — from "Time Blossoming 1"

> or time is a perpetual
> pulse of ethereal daylight,
> poetry as such surging over anyhow
> the universe with some blue ether
> the light for which nothing is impervious,
> infinity smiling, formed by that light—
>
> — from "Poetry Came Surging and Surging"

And also:

No way to contain the body heat of the whole of creation
infinity unfolds, channels its course full to the brim.

— from "A Day"

Many a voice in laughter
rising,
tears
gushing,
such
splendor
of cheerfulness!

— from "Musicians"

There is a wealth of such examples. These poetic words that describe how things flow and undulate on end, brimming over the linguistic boundary, also pervade Chong's consistent praises for nature. There's no boundary in nature's space-time as he sees. And man, by dividing time and allotting space, eventually attempts to throw things in the prison of meanings. When he sings,

Let us consider: truth is,
we bustle around
in thrall to money and machinery
spending Time like cash, like stuff,
apparently never feeling Time itself!

so one wonders what's become
of Time itself, the very flower of it
— from "Time Blossoming 2"

it is a reminder that man has assumed the ownership of time, fragmented and flittered it away, thus turning himself a slave. A life of keeping spending time, incapable of feeling it, is similar to one that has conquered nature only to lose it. Of such a life, says Chong, "we must be total wrecks / living without knowing of our own wreckage / in this world already wrecked." His 'time blossoming' perhaps denotes the flower blossoming only when one feels time itself (Time Blossoming 2), and that points to the 'daylight' flowing from beyond artificially marked time.

Nature undulating and surging beyond the world, which is divided by forced meanings, awakes Chong's mind and heart, and eventually his body. His dream poetry, or life, as sung in the following, is a life steeped in nature's blue-and-red daylight, himself flowing alongside; in this life his whole being melds into the daylight.

The ivy runners have so soon turned red!
Isn't life worth living, my heart
throbs along with these scarlet runners!
The scarlet spirits of pomegranate and apple
and of all flames flock over
to paint them so;

all spirits of the world's heart
at once invade
—"from "Scarlet Ivy Runners"

When one walks out of his room
into the wood, how happy
to hear birds singing and wheeling on their wing!
Breathing the same air they breathe
you are thoroughly one with them,
sharing the same ground with them
your motion joins theirs,
all things in one flow
shaping an infinite exterior…
—"Infinite Exterior"

The instant Chong Hyon-Jong is thoroughly in one flow with all things, throbbing through the course, steeped in nature, his being breaks forth toward the 'infinite exterior,' a gift from nature's daylight. Amid the epiphany wide open with no border between the interior and exterior, his mind overflows beyond the world's exterior. The infinite exterior he dreams of is a boundless one as shown in "A day is ten thousand years / a moment veritably an aeon. / The wind's chest is limitless / and so are the river's sighs. / The sky with all its folds / the heart with all its chambers / so goes laughter endless / as do tears" (from "A Day"). There, he escapes from the prison of meanings and sees a spectacle of things' daylight surging, throwing open his plugged senses. The daylight world seen in "not a word, and certainly no creed / but a virtual light / O the dazzle of diamond" (from "O the Dazzle of Diamond") parallels what he used to see in childhood: "This day is so fair / dusk is in its own color / sky in its own color / clouds in their own color / and these are the cumulus clouds / that I used to see as a child" (O My Hearts). It is not a world only of indicative objects, cloaked by meanings and indicated by language, but one where all things diffuse their own light. Therefore, a world of sheer senses of childhood when all things existed in their proper light, fragrance, sound, touch and taste. And a world of play and game. The ability to transform things into playthings, irrelevant to their functional use, is not this nature's great ability relished by children, who are closer to innocent nature than artificial civilization? As he sings "The heart's nature / (which is a serious play instinct) / glides past / the world's systems / and morals, / unfolds one by one / the hidden worlds" (from "The Hand Lifted in the Air"), Chong's mind flows alongside nature and enters into his childhood world, ravaged now by man-made systems and morals. Casting off all the civilization's heaps that worldly systems and morals placed in his life, Chong, as light as a ballerina standing on the surface of the earth by the smallest of her body parts, or a springy ball constantly springing over the earth, is now ready to return to an idle world of his childhood, all simple and ignorant and pure.

3. Where Poetry Dawns

Chong Hyon Jong's dream of daylight world signifies an attainment of the lightest and simplest beauty, as in some of Picasso's paintings in which the artist abstracts the object's essence with the stroke of a few lines. This is the ambitious ultimate goal to go beyond the image of an object, shaped in human consciousness not by consciousness itself but intuition, and thereby to attain the sensation of the object. In terms of phenomenology, a phenomenon is restored and its essence grasped by surpassing the actuality. Not the image of things, but the daylight flowing from things themselves takes him to where 'dawn rises" ("Time Blossoming 1") and things are created, begin to exist. Like wind or water in perpetual motion, the daylight undulates upon the perpetual beginning, and the perpetual now. In the morning world as he sings "In the morning / there's no such thing as fate. / The only thing there is / is a newborn day / with fresh vigor! "("Morning"), the now continues to flow into the then, and, instead of shaping man's fate and history, dissolves into the 'status quo" that glimmers in the moment's eternity.

Human history, nonetheless, is depleted of daylight of things and consequently fraught with all sorts of grievances. Man in his foolishness ruined the world in order to lord over it. Worse, he also ruined himself in order to survive in the ruined world. Human world perceived by Chong is a hell caught in this vicious circle.

This person
ever since his birth
turned his place into a hell.
And to lord over hell
he had to turn that place even more infernal,
for that is how to retain the hell
and what the power instinct does.

[...]

This person
shunned and hid from
the light of the day made by the sun, wind
and all hearts, and ah,
darkened the morning
and made heavy the evening.

— from "Hell"

Infinitely heavy is the life in this earthly hell: "oh heart, oh body, how dreadful to be heavy" ("Where the Wind Rises"). And while Chong laments life on earth that "can never shake off your own heaviness ("Where the Wind Rises"), he also says in such humor peculiar to him, "There's someone walking, fearing the earth will give under his feet. / A schoolbag in one hand / a shopping bag in the other— / This one anyhow seems so heavy-laden / O Ground, pray don't give way under his feet" ("Gait 9").

His is the language striving to kick off the world to bounce and soar up, and Chong wants to capture in his poems the charged moments when encountering not the human language but the daylight's. He endeavors to replicate in his own language the deep emotion a cricket rouses as it sings the "Word which, / let us say, / the sacred texts of all those so-called religions / put together / could never be anywhere near", or by the fish and tree-branches as they show him how they craft natural calligraphy greater than human words: "What made him a master calligrapher / was these fish's motions / and / these tree-branches / crafting in the air their own calligraphic style / all they wish." ("A Note on Art".)

But, as in "One's ambition to write poetry / by itself / is enough to kill it, / says Henri Michaux!" ("Killing Poetry"), the very moment poetry comes to him is not exactly when he decides to write. Rather, it just comes surging at an unexpected moment. Poetry, before it is written down in words, occurs at the moment when the poet's being unfolds toward infinity with no interior or exterior. In other words, poetry is already born when the poet is visited by infinity unexplained by language. Hence these poems:

> or time is a perpetual
> pulse of ethereal daylight,
> poetry as such surging over anyhow
> the universe with some blue ether
> smiling, formed by that light—

the infinity right in my eyes
the infinity suffusing my whole body
poetry as such still surging over anyhow
yet I chose to sleep on
instead of arising to set it down...
(it may well be that I no longer think
it'll be lost unless put down

— from "Poetry Came Surging and Surging"

The splendor
of the movement of Time
as the day draws to an end
in the gloaming
nothing wanting
so are solitude or seeds
one separate universe each
(which is splendor of all splendors)
could poetry, I wonder,
join in that movement.

— from "Whisper of Splendor"

Here, Chong tries to sleep on rather than write down the poetry that comes surging in his sleep, or questions if poetry could join in the splendor of the movement of time. It is because he believes that the essence of poetry precedes the act of writing, but disappears when written down, mere shadows hovering behind. In his Afterthoughts to *Call Me Mr. Star* (1978), Chong declared: "Until one reaches the state of dynamic stillness, his voltage of consciousness bursting forth brightest and love's window flung open within his emotion-space, at once having everything and nothing, a sort of crazy wealth—until then he cannot write a single poem. A poem is shaped before it is written down." I think what he means by the state of 'at once having everything and nothing' is an invisible, or unknowable world beyond linguistic boundaries. Though invisible and inexplicable, one's whole being inundated with the light waves, isn't this mysterious whisper of splendor of such an indescribable world already poetry in itself? So then the energy in crafting poetry has nothing to do with the poet's labored intention; it springs up when he and his poetry unite to be lifted by this whisper of splendor that comes out of the very depths of things. This leads to "the supreme way of all creation" which is the most ideal state of creativity, and the following verse embodies the assertion.

> When God the Creator created everything
> He did so by becoming the very thing.
> He flew with the bird
> when creating a bird,
> ran with the dog
> when making a dog,
> swam with the fish
> when creating a fish
>
> — from "The Creation"

The most ideal way of creation, according to the poem, is that the creator and the creature unite completely and move in unison. It is just as the baby in its effort to get out of narrow birth canal and the mother in labor billow together, two bodies as one. The instant creative energy reaches its high point, no language can intervene between the two. Because language is a gap, a distance. A woman's body billowing in labor, it is perhaps the most primal model of creation in hand. In this respect, the matrix of all creation is womanhood. The same goes with the poet giving birth to poetry. All poets long for womanhood. What on this earth produces more beautiful poetry than the very instant when life gives birth to life? The scene presented in the poem below, a mom and daughter walking in a time-space of great unconsciousness with no beginning, no end, linking life to life, has something of "the supreme way of all creation" as Chong says.

> A mom walks by, holding her little girl's hand.
> Prattle-prattle, goes the little one
> talk-talk, repeats the mom after her.
> Who am I.
> A thought flashes on me:
> I am born of that little girl.
> There's no beginning, no end, to it all.
>
> — from "Enormous Unconsciousness"

Who is he. He is born of that little girl! Not only he but all people are born of women, but the civilization and history created by the humans have long bent on shackling women in the prison of language. Leaving nature behind and walking into the prison of civilization, man has lost the womanhood within him. With the disappearance of the woman, paradise also disappeared from human world. Poetry is a calling for those who call for womanhood nonexistent in the midst of this advanced civilization, a vast stretch of graveyards. Before humans are distinguished as 'I' or 'you,' before they divide the world only to be shackled inside the bounds, poetry lives in a realm of orbed vowels replete with womanhood. Dreaming of a world of infinite light waves, Chong Hyon-Jong's poems sail up against the waters of time toward womanhood that first begot the world, toward that lost 'time blossoming.'

Well I know women.
That means I know what womanhood means.
Women are Nature.

We cannot but glory in
our Nature,
the paradise personified, said to be lost.
The matrix
which was
before history
before civilization
before me
before you,
or

as declared by André Breton:
"the corolla dripping with vowels."
— "Women"

About the Author

Chong Hyon-Jong was born in Seoul, Korea, in 1939, graduated from Yonsei University with a major in philosophy, and made his debut as a poet through "Hyondae Munhak" in 1965. His poetry books include *Dreams of Things, Call Me Mr. Star, Like a Ball Bouncing upon Falling, Not Much Time to Love, A Flower, The World's Trees, Thirst as well as a Fountain, Can't Bear It*; collections of poetry books *Feast of Pain, There's an Island between People, Dew*; collections of poetic criticism and prose *Let's Fly, My Gloomy Soul, Breath and Dreams, Magnificent Life*. He also translated several literary books into Korean.

About the Translator

Cho Young-Shil is the translator of three Korean poetry collections: *One Day, Then Another* by Kim Kwang-Kyu (White Pine Press, 2013), *A Warm Family* by Kim Hu-Ran (Codhill Press, 2014), *A Lion at Three in the Morning* by Nam Jin-Woo (Homa & Sekey Books, 2017).

She wrote *Flowers Going to Seeds*, a book of poems in memoriam of her mother (1908-2001), and in her spare time writes poems for young adults.

www.ingramcontent.com/pod-product-compliance
Lightning Source LLC
Chambersburg PA
CBHW021345090426
42742CB00008B/749

* 9 7 8 1 6 2 2 4 6 0 4 5 8 *